World Religions

CHRISTIANITY

DiscoverRoo
An Imprint of Pop!
popbooksonline.com

by Elizabeth Andrews

WELCOME TO DiscoverRoo!

This book is filled with videos, puzzles, games, and more! Scan the QR codes* while you read, or visit the website below to make this book pop.

popbooksonline.com/christianity

---

abdobooks.com

Published by Pop!, a division of ABDO, PO Box 398166, Minneapolis, Minnesota 55439. Copyright © 2024 by Abdo Consulting Group, Inc. International copyrights reserved in all countries. No part of this book may be reproduced in any form without written permission from the publisher. DiscoverRoo™ is a trademark and logo of Pop!.

Printed in the United States of America, North Mankato, Minnesota.
052023
082023  THIS BOOK CONTAINS RECYCLED MATERIALS

Cover Photo: Shutterstock Images
Interior Photos: Shutterstock Images, Getty Images
Editor: Tyler Gieseke
Series Designer: Laura Graphenteen

Library of Congress Control Number: 2022950554

Publisher's Cataloging-in-Publication Data
Names: Andrews, Elizabeth, author.
Title: Christianity / by Elizabeth Andrews
Description: Minneapolis, Minnesota : Pop!, 2024 | Series: World religions | Includes online resources and index
Identifiers: ISBN 9781098244446 (lib. bdg.) | ISBN 9781098245146 (ebook)
Subjects: LCSH: Christianity--Doctrines--Juvenile literature. | Christianity and culture--Juvenile literature. | World religions--Juvenile literature. | Religious belief--Juvenile literature.
Classification: DDC 297--dc23

*Scanning QR codes requires a web-enabled smart device with a QR code reader app and a camera.

TABLE OF CONTENTS

CHAPTER 1
Who Was Jesus? 4

CHAPTER 2
Bible and Beliefs. 10

CHAPTER 3
Love the Sinner 16

CHAPTER 4
Sacraments and Celebrations . . . 22

Making Connections. 30
Glossary 31
Index. 32
Online Resources 32

CHAPTER 1
WHO WAS JESUS?

People follow different religions across the world. A religion is an organized practice of faith and **worship**. Christianity is the biggest religion in the world. One-third of all people follow it.

WATCH A VIDEO HERE!

DID YOU KNOW? Christianity has a gospel. Gospel means "good news" in Greek.

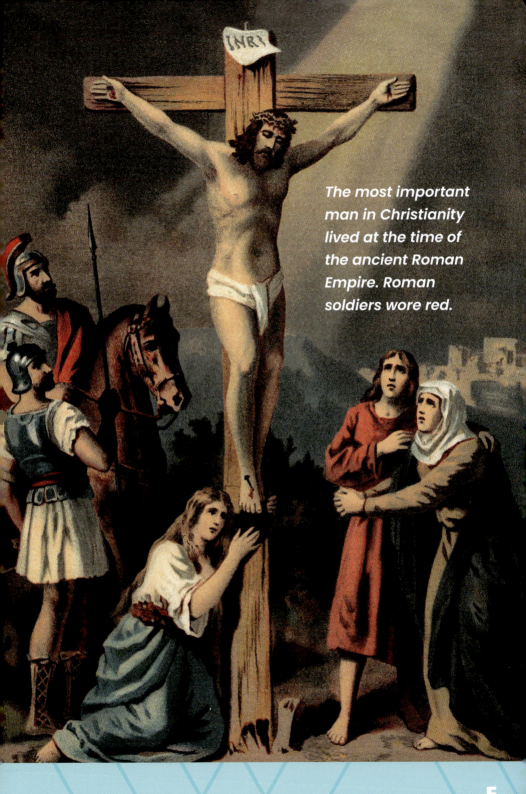

The most important man in Christianity lived at the time of the ancient Roman Empire. Roman soldiers wore red.

Jesus loved and taught all people, even the poor and sick.

Christians came from Jewish people who lived in the Middle East along the Mediterranean Sea. Jews believe in one all-powerful God. They were waiting for the **Messiah** who was predicted in the Jewish Bible.

Christians believe an angel came to Earth and told a young Jewish woman named Mary that she would give birth to the Messiah. He would be Jesus of Nazareth. Jesus was born between 6 and 4 BCE. He was the Son of God. Jesus would suffer, die, and rise from the dead to make up for people's sins.

Jesus was a real person. He began spreading his gospel with his **disciples** when he was 30 years old. Jesus wanted all people to care for one another. Jesus taught people to forgive, live good lives, and honor God. By doing this they would go to heaven when they died.

Jesus performed miracles. He healed the sick and the blind, and even raised the dead. He earned many followers. But Jesus had enemies who believed he was becoming too popular and powerful. His enemies told the Roman government of the time to **crucify** him. Jesus said his death would form a bond between humans and God.

Jesus's disciples put his body in a tomb. Christians believe he rose from the dead three

LAST SUPPER

The Last Supper was a meal shared between Jesus and his disciples the night before his crucifixion. They ate bread **symbolizing** Jesus's body. They drank wine symbolizing his blood. During the meal Jesus told his disciples one of them would betray him to the Romans.

days later. This was his resurrection. After 40 days on Earth, he rose into heaven to be with God. Jesus told his disciples to spread word of his death and resurrection. His story became the Christian faith. The cross he died upon became a symbol of Christianity.

This statue is called Christ the Redeemer *and is nearly 100 feet (30m) tall. It is located in Rio de Janeiro, Brazil.*

CHAPTER 2
BIBLE AND BELIEFS

Christians follow a book of **scripture** called the Bible. It includes the Old Testament and the New Testament. Christians believe that the words in the Bible came from God.

LEARN MORE HERE!

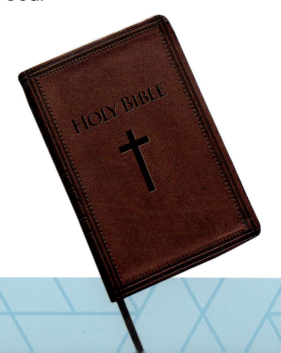

Jesus is often shown with light skin. But the real Jesus most likely had darker skin and dark curly hair.

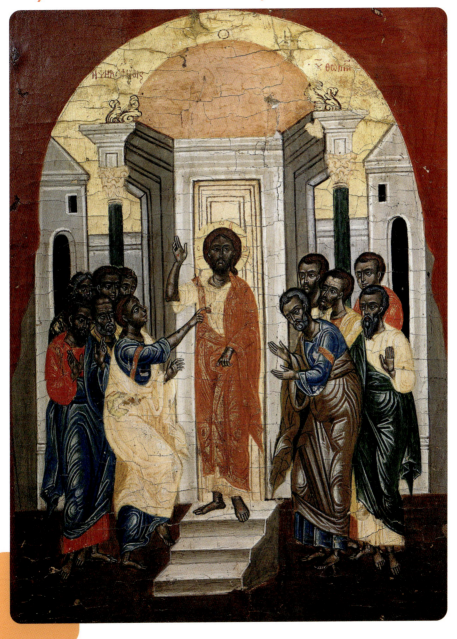

THE TEN COMMANDMENTS

1. You shall have no other gods before me.
2. You shall not take the name of the Lord your God in vain.
3. Remember the sabbath day, to keep it holy.
4. Honor your father and your mother.
5. You shall not kill.
6. You shall not commit adultery.
7. You shall not steal.
8. You shall not bear false witness against your neighbor.
9. You shall not covet your neighbor's wife.
10. You shall not covet your neighbor's goods.

The Old Testament is very similar to the Jewish Bible. It tells the story of the ancient nation of Israel. Israelites believed the one true God chose them to be his people. God gave them the Ten Commandments. These are laws that explain how to live well. The Old Testament also predicted the coming of a **Messiah**.

The New Testament was written after Jesus's death and resurrection. It tells his life story and teachings. It is believed that four of Jesus's closest followers each wrote a version of the story of Jesus.

Christians often decorate with crosses. The cross serves as a reminder that Jesus died for their sins.

Christians believe there is one God. But God is the Holy Trinity. He exists in three forms: the Father, the Son, and the Holy Spirit. God the Father is all powerful and **eternal**. He created heaven and Earth, but exists outside of them. The Son is Jesus, whom God sent to Earth to save his people. God also exists as the Holy Spirit in all his people and everywhere in the world.

Christians believe that God is perfect. Jesus also lived a perfect, sinless life.

DID YOU KNOW? Some Christians believe the Bible and its stories are **literally** true. Other Christians believe that they are just stories that lay out Christian beliefs.

The Holy Spirit is often shown as a dove.

Humans are naturally sinful. But God wants humans to live with him in heaven. When Jesus was **crucified**, he took on the punishment for all human sin. He made it possible for Christians to be judged positively when they die. This means that by avoiding sin and living well, a person can go to heaven.

CHAPTER 3
LOVE THE SINNER

A Christian's most important job is to love God completely. Another task is to love all people. To avoid sin, a Christian must treat everyone with love and kindness. Like in all religions, there are different types of Christians. Roman Catholic,

EXPLORE LINKS HERE!

Protestant, and Orthodox are three kinds. But even within these types, people practice their religion differently.

Churches can be very simple buildings, elaborate basilicas, and even megachurches the size of sports arenas.

Christians still sin even when trying to live well and follow Jesus's teachings. When that happens, they can repent. Repenting means a Christian feels bad about sinning. The Christian makes God a promise to turn away from sin the next time.

Pope Francis from Argentina became the head of the Catholic Church in 2013.

Christians follow certain practices and rituals. They go to **worship** services at a church. Services are led by church leaders. Different types of Christian leaders use different names. Deacons, priests, and bishops are Roman Catholic or Orthodox. Ministers and pastors are Protestant. All leaders believe they have been called by God to serve the Christian community.

POPE

The Pope is the head of the Roman Catholic Church. He lives in Vatican City. When a pope dies or retires, a group of church leaders called the College of Cardinals elects a new one. They vote in secret. Catholics gather outside the Vatican and wait to see black or white smoke rise from its chimney. White smoke means a new pope has been chosen. Black smoke means no cardinal earned enough votes.

Singing in Christian churches is very popular. The songs are called hymns.

Most worship services include readings from the Bible. A leader will deliver a message about a certain reading. These are called sermons or homilies. They usually include lessons about how to be a good Christian.

People at church also pray. This is when Christians have a conversation with God. Sometimes worship leaders say the prayer. Other times, individuals will say it silently to themselves. A church service is a time when Christians can repent of their sins and ask God for forgiveness.

Some church leaders wear an accessory called a collar.

DID YOU KNOW? Many Christians consider singing in church to be praying twice, once with words and again with music!

CHAPTER 4

SACRAMENTS AND CELEBRATIONS

Christian sacraments are practices that provide **spiritual blessings** to followers. Different types of Christianity perform sacraments in different ways, but the sacraments all hold similar meanings.

COMPLETE AN ACTIVITY HERE!

In Peru, people will dance for joy to celebrate Jesus coming back to life.

A man named John the Baptist baptized Jesus. John continued to travel and baptize people after.

A baptism is a **symbol** of a person's decision to turn away from sin and follow Jesus. A church leader repeats words spoken by Jesus and washes the person with water. Babies often receive baptism, but followers can also be baptized when they are older.

Another sacrament is Holy Communion. This ritual could happen at each service or only on special occasions. It is symbolic of the Last Supper Jesus had with his **disciples**. During communion, Christians eat bread and drink wine that has been blessed by the church leader. The leader speaks words that Jesus spoke when he shared the bread and wine with his disciples.

Communion bread is usually light and dry like a wafer.

Churches may decorate with beautiful flowers and fancy trees for Christmas.

Christmas and Easter are Christianity's main holidays. Christmas celebrates the day Jesus was born. It is usually observed on December 25. Some Christmas traditions include decorating a tree, going to church services, and exchanging gifts.

Lighting candles for Christmas represents the bright star in the sky people saw when Jesus was born.

Easter is the most important holiday. It honors the death and resurrection of Jesus. Many Christians go to multiple church services over a four-day period. They may also celebrate with parades or visit the graves of loved ones.

Christianity is the most popular religion in the world. Christians are united under the belief that Jesus lived and died for them. But it is a religion that allows people to practice it in their own special ways.

The barn scene with Jesus, Mary, and Joseph that people display during Christmas is called the Nativity Scene.

Many churches have beautiful windows made of stained glass.

MAKING CONNECTIONS

TEXT-TO-SELF

What part of Christianity are you most curious about? Please explain your answer.

TEXT-TO-TEXT

Have you read books about different religions? How were those religions similar to or different from Christianity?

TEXT-TO-WORLD

Do you think the world can still learn from Jesus's teachings on caring for the poor and sick? Please explain your answer.

GLOSSARY

blessing — a special gift given by God that can bring happiness or good fortune.

crucify — put someone to death by nailing or binding them to a cross, especially as an ancient punishment.

disciple — one who follows Jesus and his teachings. Jesus had 12 main disciples when he was alive.

eternal — lasting forever.

literally — in fact, exactly, or really.

Messiah — according to Old Testament predictions, a savior of the Jewish people.

scripture — any writing from the Holy Bible.

spiritual — having to do with religious matters or people's beliefs in things such as the soul or what happens after death.

symbol — an object or mark that stands for an idea.

worship — love, respect, and affection shown to an object, person, or being.

INDEX

church leaders, 19–21, 24–25
crucifixion, 8, 15

God, 6–10, 12–16, 18–19, 21

heaven, 7, 9, 14–15
holidays, 27–28
Holy Bible, 10, 13–14, 20
Holy Spirit, 14

Jesus, 7–9, 13–15, 24–25, 27–28
Jews, 6–8, 13

Pope, 19
practices, 19–20, 22, 24–25, 27–28

resurrection, 9, 13, 28
Romans, 8

sin, 7–8, 14–16, 18, 21, 24

types of Christianity, 16–17

worship, 4, 19–20

DiscoverRoo! ONLINE RESOURCES

This book is filled with videos, puzzles, games, and more! Scan the QR codes* while you read, or visit the website below to make this book pop.

popbooksonline.com/christianity

*Scanning QR codes requires a web-enabled smart device with a QR code reader app and a camera.